Alaska Wildlife

Animals & Mammals

Billy Grinslott & Kinsey Marie Books

ISBN - 9781965098776

Flying Squirrels don't fly like birds. They don't have wings. They have skin that is attached to their legs. When they jump from a tree, they spread their legs out and glide through the air. Most glides are 30 feet from tree to tree. But they can glide up to 150 feet.

Red squirrels are highly agile and can rotate their hind feet 180 degrees to climb down trees headfirst, showcasing their incredible dexterity. Their double-jointed ankles allow them to grip precarious branches and leap between trees with confidence. While known as red squirrels, their fur can also be grey-brown or rusty red. Unlike some other squirrel species, red squirrels do not hibernate during the winter but remain active, foraging for food and storing it for later.

Arctic ground squirrels are the largest ground squirrel in North America. During the cold temperatures, they can spend up to nine months in hibernation. They are the only known vertebrate that can survive body temperatures that drop below freezing while hibernating. They store food in their burrows during the summer for use in the spring when they wake up from hibernation. They are part of the Sciuridae family, which includes marmots, chipmunks, and prairie dogs. They are one of the only squirrels that can survive frigid temperatures.

The Arctic hare survives the cold temperatures with a thick coat of fur. The black fur on the ears keeps its ears warm when the sun is shining. They have black eyelashes which protect its eyes from sun glare during the winter. Arctic hares are larger than rabbits. They have taller hind legs and longer ears. Arctic hares can run up to 40 miles an hour. In winter, they sport a brilliant white coat that provides excellent camouflage in the land of ice and snow.

Marmots can't see very far. They are most active during the day because of their poor eyesight. They like to come out of their dens in the morning and afternoon. Marmots have rough fur, small ears, and short tails. Their strong feet and claws are built for digging holes in the dirt. They are nicknamed the whistle pig, for the high-pitched chirp they make to warn other group members of potential Danger.

Though the pika looks more like a mouse, it's related to the rabbit. Pikas live in colonies, with other pikas. When they sense danger, they will let out a shrill whistle to let other pikas know that there is danger. Unlike other mammals, pikas don't hibernate in the winter. Pikas are adapted to live in rocky, alpine environments at high elevations, above the tree line.

Groundhogs or woodchucks are the largest member of the squirrel family. Groundhogs get their name because of their big bodies, and they live underground. Groundhogs are skilled climbers and swimmers. Groundhogs are true hibernators, sleeping for up to six months. Groundhog Day is where Punxsutawney Phil predicts how long winter will last.

The American Mink lives across most of North America and is a cat sized. Mink are very skilled climbers and swimmers. They prefer to keep to themselves. They communicate using odors, visual signals, and other sounds. They purr when they're happy. Mink are agile swimmers, and they often dive to find food

Martens live in a variety of habitats, including forests, woodlands, and snowy areas. Martens can be distinguished from fishers, because martens are smaller, have orange on their throats and chests, and have pointier ears and snouts. Martens are part of the weasel family. They are very rare and hard to find. Their tail is long, about two thirds of their body size. There are 13 subspecies of American marten that are native to North America.

Fishers live in the forests of Canada and the northern United States. They hiss and growl when upset. They are closely related to badgers, mink, and otters. Fisher young are known as kits. Fishers are one of the few animals that eat porcupines. Fishers are also called pekan, pequam, wejack, and woolang.

The least weasel is the smallest carnivore in North America, weighing only 1 to 2.5 ounces and measuring about 6 to 8 inches long. They can be found in a variety of habitats, including forests, woodlands, grasslands, and brushy fields. Their fur is soft and dense, with brown fur on top and white fur on the underside, including the chin and feet. Weasels are clever and highly intelligent.

The Stoat is part of the weasel family. Stoats can thrive in many climates and environments. They can live in most habitats if there's food and shelter. Stoats are opportunistic predators that hunt day and night. They have a strong sense of smell and can travel up to 1.5 miles in a few hours. Stoats are good at climbing trees. They can swim and dive underwater. Stoats can reach speeds of up to 20 miles an hour. In colder climates, stoats turn almost completely white, with just a black tip on their tail.

Porcupines have sharp quills to help protect them. A porcupine can have up to 30 thousand quills, they are sharp and will stick you if you touch them. Porcupines are excellent climbers with long claws. Porcupines are shy, nocturnal, and solitary animals that spend much of their time in trees. To communicate they make grunts and high-pitched noises. A group of porcupines is called a family.

Wolverines are 30–50 inches long, with a tail of 7–10 inches. They weigh 25–60 pounds. A wolverine's color patterns are unique. No wolverine has the same fur color as another. Wolverines don't hibernate in the winter. They sleep in caves, rock crevices, or under fallen trees. Wolverines have a keen sense of smell that can detect another animal 20 feet under the snow. Wolverines have poor eyesight and are active at night. Wolverine babies are called kits. They are born with white fur that turns brown as they age.

Muskrats are found in marshes, ponds, and streams with abundant aquatic vegetation. Muskrats have a scaly tail that acts as a rudder for swimming and helps them stay afloat. They primarily eat aquatic plants like cattails, sedges, and grasses, but also consume small animals like mussels, crayfish, and fish. They have a second set of lips that close behind their front incisors, enabling them to dive underwater, chew, and eat without swallowing water. They build lodges made of mud and vegetation, and also live in burrows along the banks of water sources.

Beavers use their teeth to cut and knock down trees. They build dams with them to block water, so they have a place to live and swim. They also eat wood. Beavers can stay underwater for about 8 minutes. Beavers slap their tails on the water to indicate danger. Beavers are the largest rodents in North America.

Sea otters have the thickest fur of any animal. They have about 1 million hairs per square inch. We have 100,000 hairs on our entire head. The otter is one of the few mammals that use tools. They live between 15 and 20 years. A group of sea otters resting together is called a raft. Sea otters wrap their pups and themselves in kelp to keep from drifting out to sea. Sea otters primarily rely on their sense of touch, whiskers and forepaws, in murky waters to locate food. Sea otters have built in pouches of loose skin under their forearms to stash extra food when diving.

The Lynx is larger than the bobcat and has lighter fur and more spots. The lynx is more than twice the size of a house cat. Lynx have natural snowshoes for feet because they have long hair on their feet. Lynx like to hunt at night. They have excellent hearing and eyesight, and can spot a mouse from 250 feet away. Lynx have colors that help them blend into their surroundings. Each lynx has a different pattern, similar to a human fingerprint.

The arctic fox with its thick fur can endure temperatures that reach -90 degrees. Being able to survive in such cold weather makes it a great animal for living on the Arctic tundra and pack ice. The arctic fox does not hibernate, their fur changes colors with the seasons. The Arctic fox is the smallest member of the dog family, it's about the size of a large house cat. They live in burrows, with extensive tunnel systems.

Red foxes have excellent hearing, allowing them to hear rodents digging underground from miles away. When afraid, red foxes grin or look like they are smiling. Red foxes front paws have five toes, while their hind feet only have four. Foxes dig underground dens where they raise their kits and hide from predators. A group of foxes is called a skulk or a leash. Babys are called kits and females are called vixens.

The coyote is bigger than a fox weighing between 20 and 45 pounds. Eastern coyotes are part wolf. Coyotes are great for pest control. They like to eat mice and rats. They can adapt and live almost anywhere, even in the city. Coyotes are very smart and have been observed learning and following traffic signals in some cities. They have a yip type of call when they communicate with each other. Coyotes are found in all the United States, except Hawaii.

Wolves, coyotes, and foxes are all part of the dog family. The gray wolf is the largest wolf in North America. Wolves are legendary because of their spine-tingling howl, which they use to communicate. Each wolf has its own unique howl. Wolves are born deaf and blind, but their senses develop at about two weeks. They like to roam in packs of 2 to 25 wolves. Their territory size is 25 to 150 square miles. You can see gray and red wolves in many areas of North America.

Arctic wolves have two thick layers of fur. The outer layer gets thicker in the winter months. As a result, their body temperature can stay warm enough even when it is bitter cold outside. Arctic wolves have white fur all year which allows them to blend into their snowy surroundings. They have fur on the paws to insulate them from snow and ice and it also provides for a better grip on slippery surfaces. Arctic wolves have keen senses of sight, hearing, and smell. Arctic wolves live in packs of just a couple members to about twenty.

There are six different subspecies of moose. Moose are built for cold areas and like living in cold regions with snow. Moose are the largest members of the deer family. Moose are huge and weigh up to 1500 pounds. Moose love water and are good swimmers. Moose have poor eyesight but compensate with a good sense of smell and hearing. At 5 days old they can outrun a person.

Mountain goats can jump 12 feet in one leap. They like to live in high altitude environments. A mountain goats fur coat has a double layer that sheds in the summer and provides warmth in the winter. They have hooves designed to grip onto rocks to keep from falling. Both male and female mountain goats have horns. You can tell a mountain goat's age by counting the rings on its horns.

Dall sheep are the northernmost wild sheep in the world. The body of Dall sheep is covered with a white woolly coat that provides protection against low temperatures. Both males and females have horns. They are curved and tan in color. Their horns take up to 8 years to grow. The age of the sheep can be calculated from the number of growth rings on their horns. Dall sheep spend most of their lives on the jagged slopes of mountains. Their cloven hooves with rough pads help them cling to cliff edges and broken ledges.

Elk are the second largest members of the deer family. Bulls can weigh up to 1,100 lbs. Elk antlers can grow up to an inch per day. They can run 40 miles per hour and outrun horses. Elk have a good sense of hearing and can swivel their ears back and forth. Elk have eyes on the sides of their heads and can see in every direction except directly in front or behind. They make a cool bugling sound when communicating with other elk. It's fun to listen to them.

The musk ox gets its name from the strong, musky smell that they release. These mammals have a double coat of fur to keep them warm. Musk oxen are native to the Arctic and are well-adapted to living in the frozen tundra. Musk ox are very smart animals. They're related to sheep and goats. Musk Ox use their strong hoofed feet to dig into the icy ground for grass and plants growing on the frozen tundra. Musk oxen live in groups called herds. When threatened, musk oxen gather in a circle with their heads facing out. Their babies are protected in the middle of the circle.

Sitka deer, also known as Sitka black-tailed deer, are a subspecies of mule deer. They are native to the wet coastal rainforests of Southeast Alaska and north-coastal British Columbia. They are known for their smaller size compared to other mule deer subspecies and their ability to swim. Sitka deer primarily eat green vegetation. During the intense Alaskan winters, they also feed on woody vegetation and lichens.

Wood bison are a subspecies of the American bison. Wood bison are the largest land mammal in North America, with males weighing up to 2,000 pounds and females around 1,000 pounds. They possess a thick winter coat of fur, thick skin, and fatty tissue, allowing them to thrive in cold climates. Bison are so well insulated that the snow that falls on their coats melts off due to sunlight rather than their body heat. Wood bison are social animals, living in groups of cows and young bison, while adult bulls often live separately.

The Porcupine caribou is a herd or ecotype of the mainland barren-ground caribou the subspecies of the reindeer or caribou found in Alaska. They got their name because their birthing grounds are along the Porcupine River. They are smaller than normal caribou with a weight of around 350-400 pounds. But some have grown bigger than that. The Porcupine Caribou Herd's range covers over 150,000 square miles of northern tundra between Alaska, the Yukon and the Northwest Territories.

Caribou are also known as reindeer. Both male and female reindeer grow antlers. Reindeer are covered in hair from their nose to the bottom of their hooves. They have large, hollow hooves that help them walk on snow and dig for food. Reindeer have hair completely covering their nose. Reindeer are the only deer species to be widely domesticated. Santa uses Reindeer to pull his slay. Rudolph the reindeer is the most popular of the reindeer.

Black bears are the smallest members of the bear family in North America. Black Bears love to eat sweet things like berries, fruits, and vegetables. They are good climbers and fast runners. They are excellent swimmers and can paddle at least a mile and a half in freshwater. They usually sleep for long periods of time and hibernate during the winter. They typically try to stay away from people unless they find food in the area.

Brown bears can be up to seven feet tall and weigh up to 700 pounds for males and 350 pounds for females. Brown bears eat mostly grass, roots, and berries but will eat fish and other small mammals. They are commonly silent but can communicate with grunts, roars, or squeals.

Grizzly bears are a subspecies of the brown bear. They are called Grizzly bears because they have silver tips on their hair, a grizzled look. The hump on a Grizzly bear's back is a huge muscle. Grizzly bears don't hibernate like other bears. They are highly intelligent, have excellent memories and great smell. They are good swimmers and fast runners.

The Polar Bear is one of the biggest bears on earth. Male polar bears can weigh up to 1500 lbs. Female polar bears weigh about half as much as males. They like swimming and can swim constantly for days at a time. Polar bears keep warm thanks to the blubber or fat layer under their skin. They can smell up to a mile away. Polar bears spend most of their time at sea. They can run 25 mph, and they can swim up to 10 mph. There's still a debate of whether the Kodiak bear or the polar bear is the biggest bear in the world. Polar bears are found in Alaska and arctic areas.

Fun Facts About Alaska Animals

1 - The moose is the largest member of the deer family and can weigh up to 1,600 pounds.

2 - More than 900,000 caribou roam across vast tundra landscapes in 32 herds.

3 - Alaska has the highest concentration of bald eagles in the United States, with approximately 30,000 birds residing in the state.

4 - Alaska has 32 species of carnivores, more than any other state.

5 - Arctic mammals have developed shorter extremities to protect them from the elements.

6 - The wolverine has a reputation of being so ferocious that it can harass and run off a Grizzly Bear.

7 - Alaska is home to polar bears, brown bears, and black bears.

Author Page

Billy Grinslott & Kinsey Marie Books

ISBN – ISBN - 9781965098776

Thanks

www.ingramcontent.com/pod-product-compliance
Lightning Source LLC
Chambersburg PA
CBHW060853270326
41934CB00002B/115